CAROLYNE ROEHM

Spring

NOTEBOOK

FIRST EDITION

Library of Congress Cataloging-in-Publication Data
has been applied for.

ISBN 0-06-019453-7
00 01 02 03 04 /HK 10 9 8 7 6 5 4 3 2

CAROLYNE ROEHM

Spring

NOTEBOOK

Garden Hearth Traditions Home

PHOTOGRAPHY BY
SYLVIE BECQUET   ALAN RICHARDSON

DESIGN BY DINA DELL'ARCIPRETE-HOUSER   WRITTEN WITH MELISSA DAVIS

HarperCollins*Publishers*

welcome to the
NOTEBOOK

The first sign of spring—a robin pulling worms from the moist ground or the appearance of the first crocus—always fills my soul with the expectation of renewal. It is true that the arrival of spring is expected, but each year I am taken by surprise at the earth's willingness to get out of bed and start anew. After the long winter, I am just as eager as the plants to feel the sun and spring rain on my face, to push my fingers through the rich soil. The anticipation of things to come starts with the appearance of hellebores in late winter. By the time the apple blossoms, daffodils, and, finally, tulips arrive, I am overwhelmed by spectacular beauty . . . and a huge list of chores. Hundreds of hardy seedlings of lettuce, parsley, broccoli, chard, onion, leek, and kale leave the comfort of the cold frame to be planted in the potager. Lawn furniture is brought out of storage and dusted of cobwebs. Perennial weeds like dandelions, thistles, and pokeweed need yanking from beds and borders before they get a foothold. Peonies must be staked or spring rains will push their faces into the ground. Harvesting begins. Daily cuttings of asparagus and rhubarb mean that the kitchen is humming with new inventions. Mother's Day and Easter celebrations need to be planned and rooms made ready for visitors. In the midst of all these activities, Weatherstone is being rebuilt, so this particular spring will be one of the busiest times in my life. As workmen hammer away, I will be equally busy on my hands and knees, bringing back to life my old faithful companions. As each bloom arrives, further affirming the arrival of spring, my worries will dissipate. With the rebirth of this garden comes the rebirth of a new chapter in my life.

CONTENTS

Spring

DAFFODILS

I have never thought much of daffodils in beds; they look too constrained and orderly. I like lakes of daffs spilling across a meadow, or scrambling over a hillside, or running amok through an abandoned farmyard. This was the picture I had in my mind when I decided to plant daffodils in the orchard meadow at Weatherstone. I vaguely knew that if I planted good fat bulbs, they would eventually duplicate with no help from me, and I would someday achieve the picture in my head of sweeps of sunlit flow–ers. That first fall I dug in a few hundred bulbs, but it was not enough—a trickle, not a flood. The second year I was bolder and added ten times as many, but still, it was not enough. I was growing patient in inverse proportion to the daffs' willingness to cooperate with my plan. Time to step up the action and actually read a bulb book. I estimated that I would need to fill about an acre of the meadow. An acre is 43,560 square feet. The planting guide suggested 2 bulbs per square foot, or about 87,000 bulbs. If I bought in bulk, the best I could do was $300 per thousand bulbs. Needless to say, I would not be having my instant acre of daffodils. I would have to be patient and let the bulbs multiply at their own rate. I would have to let them naturalize.

Although daffodils show well in formal borders and beds, their impact is best appreciated in a natural setting: under a grove of deciduous trees, in front of an unpruned gathering of shrubs, or in streamlike swaths drifting through a meadow. Daffs grow well in USDA Zones 3 through 8, accept full sun or partial shade, and are not picky about soil pH, so it is not difficult to find a spot for them in the landscape. Once an appropriate site has been chosen, bulbs must be ordered and planted quickly soon after delivery; bulbs lose their vigor if stored too long. Bulbs are ordered in late summer, arrive in fall, and should be planted at least four weeks before the ground freezes. Remember that when you are choosing bulbs, size does matter. The bulb contains the food that produces the bloom, so do not hesitate to invest in larger bulbs.

"AND THEN MY HEART WITH PLEASURE FILLS, AND DANCES WITH THE DAFFODILS."

—WILLIAM WORDSWORTH

From top, left to right: Naturalized daffodils in Weatherstone's orchard—'Ice King,' 'Flower Record,' 'King Alfred,' 'Mt. Hood,' 'Martinette,' 'Mt. Hood,' 'Salome,' 'Cheerfulness,' 'Yellow Cheerfulness'

TIP

Cut daffodils are usually posed with their own kind not only because they are beautiful in a group, but also because they exude a sap that clogs the stems of other flowers and shortens their life. If you are mixing daffs with other cut flowers, trim the daff stem and hold it over a candle or gas flame to sear the end and stop the flow of sap.

personal notes:

narcissi's reflection

Each spring when the orchard meadow bursts into bloom, I hold a small lunch—half picnic, half al fresco—under the bows of the apple trees. Some years the center of the table stars a bundle of nearby assorted narcissi gathered into a rustic pot (*opposite left*). Other years I mix the flowers with other early-blooming bulbs such as *Fritillaria persica* (*above and opposite right*), a delightful deep purple relative of the lily. If I am mixing daffs with other flowers, I try to pay close attention to the combination of forms—doubles, singles, minis, and trumpets—to balance the bouquet.

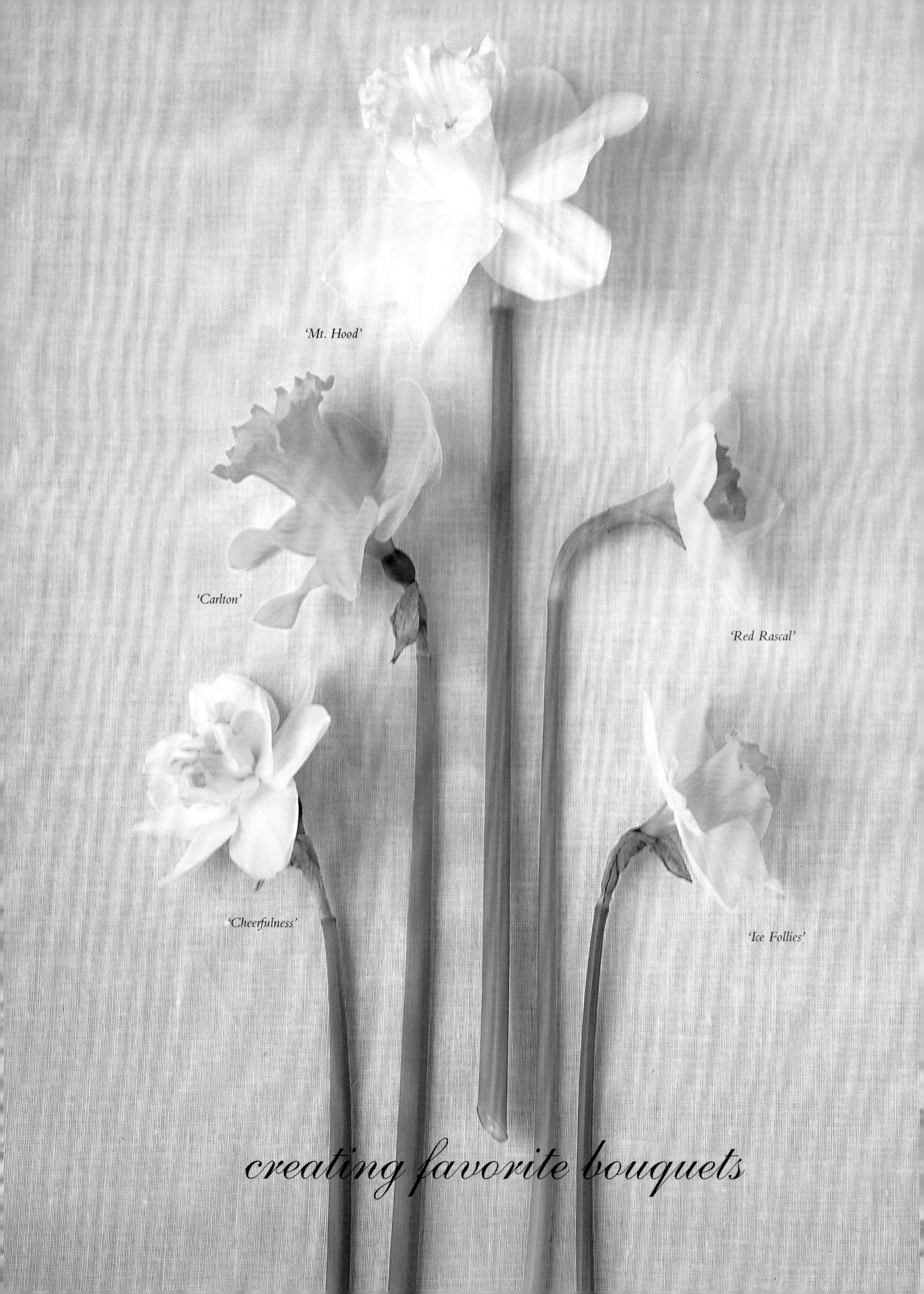

'Mt. Hood'

'Carlton'

'Red Rascal'

'Cheerfulness'

'Ice Follies'

creating favorite bouquets

Clockwise from top left: The blue-and-white vase holds 'Flower Record,' mini 'Martinette,' and poeticus daffs; forget-me-nots, tulips 'Negrita' and 'Valentines,' trollius; and euphorbia. The white pitcher is filled with a mixed gathering of triumph and tazetta narcissus. It may have once been a footbath, but the white tub now serves as a vase for a group of triumph daffs. Spring anemones and tulips brighten a sunny spring breakfast.

WEATHERSTONE NATURALIZED DAFFODILS

NAME	COLOR	TYPE	HEIGHT (INCHES)	BLOOM
Actaea	white petals, yellow cup rimmed red with green eye; fragrant	Poeticus	16"	April–May
Barrett Browning	white petals, small red-orange cup	Small Cupped	14–16"	April
Carlton	yellow petals, yellow cup	Large Cupped	16–18"	early spring
Cheerfulness	white petals, double pale yellow cup; fragrant	Double	14-16"	late spring
Delibes	yellow petals, yellow cup with orange rim	Large Cupped	18–20"	April
Duke of Windsor	white petals, orange cup	Large Cupped	18–20"	April
Flower Record	white petals, yellow cup with red trim; slight fragrance	Large Cupped	18–20"	April
Geranium	white petals, bright orange cup; fragrant	Tazetta	12–14"	mid-spring
Hawera	pale yellow petals, canary yellow cup	Trandrus	6–8"	early spring
Ice Follies	white petals, ruffled canary yellow cup	Large Cupped	16–18"	early spring
King Alfred	deep yellow petals, yellow cup	Trumpet	16–18"	early spring
Mt. Hood	ivory white petals, white cup	Trumpet	16–18"	early spring
Orange Progress	golden yellow petals, orange cup	Large Cupped	16–18"	mid-spring
Peeping Tom	yellow petals, yellow cup	Cyclamineus	14–16"	early to late spring
Red Rascal	yellow petals, orange-red cup; fragrant	Large Cupped	18–20"	early spring
Salome	white petals, pink cup	Large Cupped	14–16"	mid-spring
Scarlet Gem	yellow petals, orange-red cup with green eye	Tazetta	14–16"	April
Spellbinder	yellow petals, cream cup	Trumpet	18–20"	April
Tête-à-Tête	golden yellow petals with darker cup	Cyclamineus	6–7"	April
Unsurpassable	yellow petals, yellow cup	Trumpet	16–18"	early spring

EASTER

When I was growing up, Easter was filled with comforting ritual. My parents would give me a live baby chick—artificially dyed pastel blue, lilac, or green—purchased from the dime store. My grandmother and I would tint oversized goose eggs taken from her henhouse to fill the Easter basket. I was usually given a stuffed toy, my favorite being a purple bunny with real white rabbit–fur ears. Best of all was shopping for the Easter Sunday outfit: new hat, shoes, coat, dress, and white cotton gloves that I would gnaw the tips off of. Although it has been some time since I have put on an Easter bonnet, I still borrow from some of those memories to create my own Easter celebration. When looking for a theme for my decorations, a candy box, a silk ribbon, or a nosegay of violets at the farmer's market can inspire me. Whenever I travel, I keep an eye out for unusual miniature objects to decorate holiday tables. For Easter, I scout out whimsical egg cups (easy to collect because a matched set is unnecessary) for displaying fanciful colored eggs or to fill with a few spring flowers. I also try to find small baskets and vases to use in miniature versions of larger arrangements or to complement a breakfast tray. My newer acquisitions may not have the same gravitas as the childhood dyed chicks, but they have taken on their own traditions. Every year the ear falls off one of my thatched bunnies and I have to reattach it with the glue gun. The surgery is a strange, but comforting, ritual.

bBlue and white is a perennial color theme for me, so I was delighted to find these very inexpensive blue-and-white-painted eggs, based on the Russian art of *pisanki* (*opposite*). The eggs were a perfect foil for the blue-and-white export and Delft china and the simple bouquet of orange-cupped daffodils and electric-blue forget-me-nots (*below*). I often mix reproduction blue-and-white china with a few good pieces of Chinese export to stretch my collection. The present is wrapped in white freezer paper, tied with a blue-and-white-checked ribbon, and topped with a single sprig of lily of the valley.

Left: I covered a vase in reverse camellia leaves tied with raffia and filled it with ranunculus and pansies. The tiny basket on the Easter breakfast tray contains marbleized jelly beans, both objects playing off the theme of the larger basket. I added tiny papier-mâché baskets with daffodils poked into small floral picks, which were camouflaged by the straw (*above*).

Right: I designed this basket for a country table, and filled it with small thatched bunnies I found in a Parisian street market. Natural hen eggs and tiny mottled brown quail eggs are nestled in a bed of straw.

a country lunch

I found this rustic wooden box filled with terra-cotta pots at a local flea market and was so taken with its aged patina that I made it the center of my Easter lunch in the country. I filled half of the pots with daffodils, and the other half with rye grass from the florist. I used the same grass to blanket the myrtle topiaries. To mark the places, I stuffed a small clay pot with sphagnum moss, wrote the guest's name on the egg with a laundry marker, and placed the egg on the moss nest.

I save greeting cards and postcards and recycle them as gift tags (*right*). The ivy-covered topiary basket (*below*) came from a florist in New York (it is widely available elsewhere). I filled the basket with a sugared bunny I brought home from a *confiseur* in Paris and eggs from the Weatherstone henhouse, which I rolled in sugar to match the bunny.

TIP

To make sugared eggs at home, roll a dry hard-cooked white egg in a beaten egg white. Sprinkle with castor sugar and let dry on a paper towel.

MOTHER'S DAY

When I was four years old, I decided to use my own allowance to buy a Mother's Day gift. I wanted to give my mother her favorite perfume, Joy, but soon found that such an ambitious purchase required more than what I could shake out of my pink glass piggy bank. But I had a backup plan. My mother had often expressed her appreciation for the neighbor's tulips, so early Sunday morning I went over to their yard and picked every one. When my mother was presented with the plundered tulips she knew immediately where they came from. She explained that the neighbor's flowers were not public property, but since they were stolen out of love, I was not to be punished. I had to apologize to our neighbor, but she graciously forgave me because the tulips were pinched with the right heart. To this day, I try to show my mom the same appreciation, to thank her for taking care of me all my life, but without resorting to larceny. What my mother—and I think most moms—appreciates is a day of pampering, an act that requires more effort than money. You can begin her day by serving her a breakfast-in-bed tray accompanied by a favorite novel or newspaper, fresh tea or coffee, crisp white linens, and a sweet gathering of her favorite flowers. The Mother's Day gift can be the vase that holds the flowers, the linen place mat, the tea set, or the tray itself. Over the years you can add to the Mother's Day tray and begin a tradition, so that every year Mom will find some new object added to her tray that says: Thank you for your kindly sacrifices.

Being a pack rat has its pluses. I dove into my box of saved bits and pieces of wrapping paper and ribbons and quickly created the tray below. I cut a piece of gingham with pinking shears to fit the bottom of the tray, and wrapped the gift with a sheet of Venetian paper and silk ribbon saved from a Christmas package. I topped the box with velvet flowers I found in a thrift shop and tucked in a sprig of viburnum berries found on my morning walk. The gift tag is a packing label addressed with gold marker. I had a large basket of cherry plums delivered by a friend who was overwhelmed with fruit and added a handful to the tray in a simple white porcelain bowl. All the colors just fell together to create a charming whole. *Opposite:* Let Mom spend the rest of the day lounging, sipping iced tea while dreamily thumbing through wish books.

The Rose and the Clematis *as good companions*

VISIONS of ROSES by PETER BEALES

DAVID HICKS — COTSWOLD GARDENS

GARDENING AT SISSINGHURST Tony Lord

"WOMEN NEED REAL MOMENTS
OF SOLITUDE AND SELF-REFLECTION
TO BALANCE OUT HOW MUCH OF
OURSELVES WE GIVE AWAY."
—BARBARA DE ANGELIS

Top left: Spode's everyday china Fitzhugh Blue holds French toast. The tray needs only one or two clever elements to make it special, such as the silver egg cup (*top right*), or a wee basket holding a pansy plant, its base obscured by a fringed breakfast napkin (*top left*). The blue-and-white pitcher (*above left*) is filled with wild flowers plucked from a meadow, and accompanied by a fresh bowl of blueberries and cream. Breakfast on a tray can be a simple matter of filling a wicker basket with gift packages wrapped in grass cloth, topped with artificial acadia buds (*above right*). Or it can be more elaborate, served on a silver tray dressed with antique Wedgwood china and a silver mesh basket filled with forget-me-nots (*opposite*).

TULIPS

Tulips, more than any flower, seem to trigger the most opinionated reactions, even from the mild-mannered plantsman. One gardener I know absolutely will not grow red Darwin tulips of any kind, only pastels. Another is strongly offended by fringed and lily forms, but is bonkers over peony shapes. Still another is neurotic about his aversion to the viridiflora 'Greenland' but gets moony over the squat little greigiis, which I hate. I spend a good deal of time in July obsessing over what tulips to order for the potager. I mentally juggle permutations of bloom times, stem length, form, and color so that each potager block blooms at precisely the same time, at the same height, with the most pleasing color combination. I still haven't gotten it right. Selecting tulips for the cutting garden is a little easier on the psyche, since the flowers are grown exclusively for the vase. Like every other tulip fancier, I have my extreme loves for cutting: the riotous Rembrandts and parrots. I'm drawn to their odd streaks of craziness and their individuality—no two are the same. Looking at a bundle of painted tulips is like staring into a whirlpool of the fantastic. I wonder: How did nature decide to follow such an eccentric course? Next on my list are the ultramodern streamlined Darwins, like 'Queen of the Night' and 'Purple Prince,' which knock your socks off when paired with deep 'Orange Emperor' or the saintly white 'Maureen.' This year I've gone overboard with textures, pulled in by the feathered edges of fringed tulips, the spiky crowns of lily tulips, and the double opulence of peony tulips. Next year, who knows? There are nearly 3,000 tulips in general cultivation to choose from. And I am sure to have a strong opinion about each.

The potager squares in early spring are naked—awaiting baby lettuces and parsley—except for the tulips planted in color-block squares inside the Belgian blocks. After much trial and error, it is still a challenge to coordinate the heights, colors, and bloom times so the flower blocks look their best. The center of the larger squares holds sturdy Guy Wolff pots, which will be filled with annuals. I try not to cut the tulips in the blocks, which would disrupt the geometry of the plan, but I am eager to cut the tulips in the cutting garden, which was planted solely for that sacrifice.

personal notes:

In the cutting garden (*above*), tulips are planted tightly together so the missing flowers won't be easily noticed. Although I try not to put rows of clashing colors next to each other, the only true plan for the rows is that they hold my favorite varieties, such as 'Meissner Porzellan' (*right*).

TIP

Hybrid tulips, especially Darwins, are classified as a perennial flower, and they are in their native habitat in the foothills of the Himalayas. But in the home garden the bloom size lessens after the first year and eventually stops flowering altogether. It is best to pull the bulbs after they bloom and replace them with annuals.

"SPRING HAS COME AGAIN.
THE EARTH IS LIKE A CHILD
WHO KNOWS POEMS."

-RAINER MARIA RILKE

I have gotten to know tulips best by photographing them. You begin to see all the intricacies of the blossom when you spend hours focusing on their petals. The buds start out tight, like lined-up soldiers; then as the blossoms age, they get looser and blowsier, to reveal a kaleidoscopic black eye (*right*) just hours before the petals drop.

'Queen of the Night' and 'White Dream' (*left*) are two of my favorite color combinations to use inside the Belgian block squares. My other favorites are relegated to the cutting garden (*above*) a few feet away. By the time the tulips are pulled to be replaced by annuals, there is barely a bloom left that has not been cut.

When I flip through the bulb catalogs in summer—a blissfully long process—I look at the tulip offerings much as I look at fabric: I react to form, texture, and color. I also respond to them as a collector would, evaluating each blossom for what it can contribute to the vase, in a particular color group, irrationally ignoring the colors I don't like. I have my prejudices—I don't like the single reds and yellows overused in public parks—as I have my loves, parrots and painteds. But like any collector, my tastes shift gradually. Each season I find myself gravitating toward a form or color I had not appreciated before. Which is why I love flowers. They force you to learn.

WHEN I SELECT TULIP BULBS FOR THE CUTTING GARDEN, I THINK LIKE A COLLECTOR. I AM BUILDING A COLLECTION FOR THE VASE.

Top row: 'Attila' and the lily-shaped 'Ballade,' the red flames of 'Flair,' and the ruffles of 'Red Parrot.' *Bottom row:* 'Attila' opens its petals wide. A collection of painted, peony, and parrot tulips from the Paris flower market (also available in the States). 'Mt. Tacoma' displays all her charms.

For years I avoided the fashion of white gardens, until I built the border outside my breakfast room (*left*). I wanted a restful morning view, without the interruption of color, which would segue well into the green meadow beyond. We planted espaliered apple trees, 'Iceberg' and 'Sea Foam' roses, and white lilac for structure. 'White Dream' tulips filled the front of the bed, edged with variegated hosta 'Albomarginata,' which has thrived despite the constant exposure to sun. I also built a formal white garden (*above top*) that comes to life in early spring with white tulips (*above*), anemones, peonies, dianthus, and poppies.

dutch masters

I am not ashamed to say that I lift many bouquet ideas from the exquisite flower paintings of the seventeenth century. The arrangement below, inspired by the works of de Heem and van Ost, makes the best use of red tulips (such as 'Napa Valley,' 'Bastogne,' or 'Brawny'), viburnum flowers, the small chrysanthemum 'Kermit,' and a pink hyacinth ('Pink Lilac' or pale-pink Roman hyacinth). I chose a porcelain pedestal vase painted with the same colors as the flowers, the gold-tooled books, and the silk curtains. By borrowing from these elements, I found the bouquet fits its environment perfectly.

Top: Red-and-white parrot and painted tulips, a favorite of the Dutch masters, are matched with a few solid red Darwins and sprigs of young viburnum berries. *Bottom:* I cut four different varieties of lilacs—deep purple ('Dark Night'), medium blue ('President Lincoln'), pink ('Katherine Havemeyer') and lavender ('Victor Lemoine')—while still a bit in bud. Using pick frogs at the base of the reproduction blue-and-white bowl, I added dark maroon 'Queen of the Congo' and 'Queen of the Night,' painted 'Green Wave,' 'Sorbet' and 'Meissner Porzellan,' the lily tulip 'Ballade,' and the triumph 'Negrita.'

Top: To bring the best out of a sunny day, I chose yellow tulips streaked with red from a Rembrandt look-alike mix and added 'Texas Flame' and 'Flaming Parrot.' The daffodils include 'Actaea,' 'Barrett Browning,' 'Cheerfulness,' 'Yellow Cheerfulness,' and the Darwin tulip 'Orange Favorite.' *Bottom:* Spinning off the oranges, reds, yellows, and greens of the mangoes, I dressed a rustic luncheon table with nosegays of 'Princess Irene,' 'Arabian Night,' 'Olympic Flame,' 'Yellow Appledorn,' and a few harmonizing peony tulips from a peony mix.

A SIMPLE PITCHER OF BUDS SNIPPED FROM THE CUTTING GARDEN SHOW OFF THE BEST THAT SPRING CAN OFFER.

A dozen white 'Tacoma' tulips mix with lily of the valley and its leaves, daffodil 'Thalia,' white anenome, and spring snowflake (Leucojum vernum) to make a pure expression of innocence.

white medley

I have spent most of my adult life working with strong colors. When I was a clothing designer, I was never charmed by white and its subtle shades. I wanted impact. But now that I have gotten older, I am beginning to appreciate the quiet statement that white can make and am depending more and more on the restful color combination of green and white. I still thrill over the riot of color in the perennial border in June, but I am soothed by the green and white garden outside my breakfast room window. I think of the white 'Tacoma' tulips (*below*) as the personification of the harmony of white. It is the pearl of the garden.

WEATHERSTONE TULIP CHART

NAME	TYPE	COLOR	HEIGHT (INCHES)	BLOOM
Ad Rem	Darwin	red with yellow margin	24–26"	mid-spring
Annie Schilder	Triumph	warm orange	18"	late April
Apeldoorn	Darwin	red with a black eye	20–24"	mid-spring
Apricot Beauty	Triumph	apricot	16–18"	mid-spring
Apricot Parrot	Parrot	apricot and green	18–20"	late spring
Astarte	Triumph	deep red	16–18"	mid-spring
Atlantis	Triumph	purple with white and yellow margins	16–18"	late spring
Atlantis	Single	purple painted white	16–18"	late spring
Attila	Triumph	grape	18–20"	mid-spring
Ballade	Lily	purple and white	20–22"	late spring
Barcelona	Triumph	deep pink	18–22"	mid-spring
Barcelona	Single	rose	18–20"	mid-spring
Bastogne	Triumph	blood-red with red flames	18"	late April
Bestseller	Single	salmon-copper painted	16"	early spring
Big Chief	Darwin	rich pink	24–26"	mid-spring
Black Parrot	Darwin	purple-black fringed	20"	late spring
Blue Diamond	Peony	grape-lilac	16–18"	late spring
Blue Heron	Fringed	grape	22–24"	late spring
Blue Parrot	Parrot	grape	18–20"	late spring
Burning Heart	Darwin	white painted with red and yellow	20–24"	mid-spring
Carnaval de Rio	Triumph	red and white flames	18–20"	mid-spring
Cream Upstar	Peony	pale yellow with a rose edge	14"	late spring
Dutch Fair	Darwin	yellow with red flames	22"	mid-spring
Estella Rijnveld	Parrot	red-white	18–20"	late spring
Flair	Single	yellow with red flames	14"	early spring
Gavota	Triumph	deep purple	16–18"	mid-spring
General de Wet	Single	orange	13"	early spring
Georgette	Multiflowering	orange painted red	18–20"	late spring
Hans Anrud	Triumph	deep purple	22"	late April
High Society	Triumph	deep pink, orange edge	16–18"	mid-spring
Hollandia	Triumph	brilliant red	16–18"	mid-spring
Marathon Champion	Triumph	magenta	18–20"	mid-spring

WEATHERSTONE TULIP CHART

NAME	TYPE	COLOR	HEIGHT (INCHES)	BLOOM
Maureen	Darwin	white	28–30"	late spring
Meissner Porzellan	Triumph	pink with rose margins	18–20"	mid-spring
Monsella	Double	yellow with red stripes	12"	early spring
Montreux	Double	pale yellow with peach	10–12"	early spring
Montreux	Double	yellow with rose-red edge	12"	early spring
Mount Tacoma	Peony	white	18–20"	late spring
Napa Valley	Triumph	deep red	18–22"	mid-spring
Negrita	Triumph	deep purple	18–20"	mid-spring
New Design	Triumph	silver-pink with yellow and rose tips	20"	late April
Ollioules	Darwin	rose with a white edge	22"	mid-spring
Olympic Flame	Darwin	yellow and red painted	20–24"	mid-spring
Orange Bowl	Darwin	deep orange with yellow flames	20"	mid-spring
Orange Queen	Darwin	warm orange	20–24"	mid-spring
Parrot Mixed Colors	Parrot	mix	18–20"	late spring
Parrot Tulip Collection	Parrot	white fire, flaming, blue	20–28"	late spring
Passionale	Triumph	rose-purple	16–18"	mid-spring
Peer Gynt	Triumph	rose-pink with a silver-pink edge	20"	late spring
Peony Flowering Tulip Collection	Peony	pink, dark red, white, lilac	18–22"	late spring
Pink Impression	Darwin	mid-pink	20–24"	mid-spring
Princess Irene	Single	orange and red painted	12–14"	early spring
Purple Prince	Single	lilac, deep purple interior	20"	early spring
Queen of the Night	Giant	deep maroon-black	28–30"	late spring
Rembrandt Look-Alike Mix	Rembrandt	painted	24–26"	late spring
Rembrandt Tulips	Rembrandt	mixed	20–24"	mid- to late spring
Scarlet Majesty		red double	18–20"	mid-spring
Shirley	Triumph	white with a grape edge	18–20"	mid-spring
Swan Wings	Fringed	white	22–24"	late spring
Sweet Harmony	Darwin	medium yellow with a white edge	22–24"	late spring
Texas Flame	Parrot	yellow with red and green	18–20"	late spring
Valentine	Triumph	cherry-pink, pale edge	16–20"	mid-spring

PANSIES

When I come upon a swath of pansies on a spring morning, I often feel as if I've interrupted a party of eager children caught in the midst of some slightly devilish play. Peering closely into the center black blotch of a bicolor, I see two wide eyes and a drooping mustache under a button yellow nose. Could these be the critical grandfathers of the unruly pranksters in their midst? It does seem to be the nature of pansies that they are looking at us, rather than we at them. With their wide array of outfits—from pink ballerina tutus to somber black tuxedos—they are not self-conscious of their charms. Perhaps it is this knowing nature of the flower's expression that earned the pansy its name, a corruption of the French word *pensée,* or remembrance. • I plant pansies in pots to line the double staircase on the front facade at Weatherstone and to line the walkway of my cottage, Weatherpebble. I also plant rambling Johnny-jump-up violas, the mother of all pansies, at the foot of my roses to hide their leggy canes. In the house, I use plain potted pansies to decorate a spring breakfast table. Pansies also excel as a cut flower because—and how many flowers can you say this about—they love to be picked. The more they are plucked, which really amounts to deadheading, the more they will put out a show of bloom. However, even with the most conscientious deadheading, pansies do stop producing and become leggy by midsummer. But if the scraggly plants are cut back to half their length, they will come back into a renewed flush of bloom.

Modern pansy hybrids emerged from a long line of breeding from a group of over 500 viola species, known in Greek herbal medicine as early as the fourth century B.C. However, we have a nineteenth-century English gardener, William Thompson, to thank for the wide array of pansies available today. Thompson crossed various wild viola and selected offspring for color and showier flower size, eventually achieving the new hybrid group, *Viola wittrockiana*. Thompson continued to breed for huge blocks of color on the lower petals, called the face. Discovered in 1839 and named 'Medora,' this pansy and its offspring became popular with gardeners and breeders throughout Europe. By the turn of the century a Scottish breeder named Charles Stewart focused on breeding hybrids with more plant vigor and flowers that had no dark blocks or lines, developing pansies with clear colors and no face.

Recent hybridizers have focused on selecting for larger blooms and on extending the pansy season, creating heat-tolerant varieties such as the 'Bingo' series that can perform all summer. The largest hybrid blossoms on the market, 'Majestic Giants,' often have blossoms up to 4 inches across. These larger blooms, though impressive, suffer from severe shyness and have trouble holding up their heads. The broad blossoms can overwhelm the small plant, so blooms in the 2-inch range may be a wiser choice for spring beds.

Although most gardeners buy pansy plants from commercial growers, the flower is very easy to grow from seed started indoors in December. Pansy seed, and especially viola seed, has a very high germination rate if sown in cool conditions; a packet of 100 seeds may give you nearly that number of plants. Pansies need darkness to germinate, so the seed should be covered with about ⅛ inch of soil and given temperatures of 60° to 65°F. for strong germination, which occurs in about two weeks. Once pansies have two sets of leaves they may be planted out in the garden.

PLANTING POINTS

- *Start pansy seed indoors in December or January.*
- *Seed needs darkness to germinate.*
- *Pansies bloom best in cool weather.*
- *If buying plants, choose those not in bloom, but with tightly wrapped flower buds present.*
- *Pansies grow best with a half day of sun.*
- *Cut back plants by half in midsummer to renew blossoms.*

I line the walkway to my cottage front door with pots of various purple wittrock-iana pansies nestled next to a border of bright blue nepeta. In midsummer, when the plants become too leggy, the nepeta is cut back to a tight mound and the pansies are replaced with lobelia 'White Cascade.'

TIP

Although pansies are not noted for their scent, the yellow and blue varieties, especially, emit a delicate perfume.

I underplant my pink roses with varying shades of violas and pansies and edge the old brick walkways with deep blue-violet lobelia (*left*). I have a big tendency to crowd my terra-cotta pots (*above and opposite*) in order to create a blast of color. Deadheading helps the pansies and violas burst with bloom until mid-July.

In Paris, pansies sold in local markets are bound into nosegays collared with ivy leaves (*above*). I plant pansies in pots to line the double staircase at Weatherstone (*opposite*) and to fill the urn in the perennial garden (*right*). I always use potted flowers in the front rose garden because I like the look of mossy pots filled with a wild array of pansies.

Rose 'Gertrude Jekyll'

Rose 'Gertrude Jekyll' (bud)

Blue Frost Hybrid

Viola 'Bowles' Black'

Viola wittrockiana cultivar

Viola cultivar

Rose 'Mary Rose'

Copying the colors of the flowers on the hand-painted vase, I mix stems of 'Gertrude Jekyll' and 'Mary Rose' with an assortment of purple wittrockiana pansies.

My addiction to pansies grew immensely after a trip to Kashmir, where flower vendors sold boatloads of pansies, lilacs, and sweet peas alongside our houseboat. For a pittance I bought every bud the floating vendors offered and decorated to overflowing each room in our houseboat. I dreamed of re-creating the same scene in Connecticut, but my garden could never supply every room of my house with flowers. I am happy to settle for small beakers of velvet pansies and viola, sometimes coupled with lilacs and Jacob's Ladder (*above*), scattered around the house.

It is not difficult to understand why the pansy is called the flower of remembrance. According to flower lore, because the petals of a pansy are heart-shaped, they were thought to cure a broken heart. The ancient Celts made tea from the pansies to use as a love potion. Although I can't attest to its efficacy as a stimulant for the lovelorn, I do know that a small pot of pansies brings a smile to my face. It was a quick project to fill a silver jam jar with pansies and viola—grouped and pushed into floral picks for support—to lighten up the breakfast room table (*above*).

Birthday parties are not for adults. We don't take well to being reminded that we are getting older. A friend of mine was of such a mind, and when her birthday rolled around, I knew she would need some bolstering. I made her one of my grandmother's angel food cakes, brought out my most feminine dessert plates and watery periwinkle crystal, and draped the table in crisp white linens. Since she is a collector of teddy bears, I bought the sphagnum moss cub and tucked a birthday bibelot between its arms. We named him Mousse, French for moss. I covered a little terra-cotta pot with sheet moss and tucked a nosegay of pansies and viburnum flowers inside and filled the center of the cake with pansies. She was charmed by my small efforts and barely minded that another year had passed.

HOW TO MAKE THE MOSS-COVERED POT

Materials Needed
Small container
Sheet moss
Rubber cement or waterproof glue

How To
Any type of container will work as your vase. I used a terra-cotta pot, but you can use a plastic container, a tin can, or a glass. Be sure to use something that you won't mind being permanently covered. Because I used a terra-cotta pot, which is porous, I used a small glass to line the pot.

1. Select a piece of sheet moss that will cover your container. Clean weeds and debris from the moss and shake off excess dirt. Cut the moss in a shape that will cover your container, leaving approximately 1 ½ inches of extra moss needed to fold over the top of the container.

2. Apply rubber cement or a waterproof glue to the outside of your container so that the entire surface is covered. Carefully adhere the moss to the container (with the 1 ½ inches of extra moss at the top of the container).

3. Fold the 1 ½ -inch border at the top of the container over the rim so that it smoothly adheres to the inside of the container.

4. Trim any areas that need to be cleaned up.

In the tradition of my grandmother Beaty, I also use pansies and viola to decorate spring and early summer birthday cakes of angel food topped with fluffy royal icing. A hidden vase of flowers nests inside the center hole of the cake, poking out above the frosting. Grandmother Beaty always made these delightful cakes for my birthday in May, changing the center bouquet each year from fragrant narcissus to wild violets or pansies, depending on the state of her garden. I carry on the tradition for family and friends. This is the cake recipe that my grandmother always used for my birthday cake of angel food and royal frosting. There are probably thousands of good recipes out there, but nostalgia wins out. To this day, it is the one that I use.

23-MINUTE ANGEL FOOD CAKE
Serves 8

1½ cups egg whites
¼ teaspoon salt
1 teaspoon cream of tartar
1 cup granulated sugar
1 cup confectioners' sugar
1 cup sifted Swansdown cake flour
½ teaspoon almond extract
1 teaspoon vanilla extract

1. Preheat oven to 425° F. Heat a 10-inch ungreased tube pan in the oven while making the batter.
2. Beat egg whites with salt and cream of tartar until stiff but not dry. Sift in granulated sugar, 2 tablespoons at a time.
3. Sift flour and confectioners' sugar together 5 times. Fold the flour and confectioners' sugar by tablespoons into the egg-sugar mixture. Fold in flavoring extracts.
4. Pour batter into the hot tube pan. Bake for 23 minutes, no longer. Cool in inverted pan.

Icing

1 cup sugar
1 egg white
½ teaspoon salt
¼ teaspoon cream of tartar
½ teaspoon almond extract
½ teaspoon boiling water

Put sugar, egg white, salt, cream of tartar, and almond extract in a mixing bowl. Start mixer and add the boiling water. Beat until of spreading consistency.

MY CHILDHOOD HAPPY BIRTHDAY
CAKE: ANGEL FOOD TOPPED
WITH ROYAL ICING AND
freshly PLUCKED PANSIES

PANSY AND VIOLA FAVORITES

PANSIES

'Blues Jam Hybrid' (blue mix)

'Bingo Deep Purple' (deep purple-yellow eye)

'Burgundy Laced Picotee'

'Chalon Victorian' (deep colors, ruffled edges)

Crystal Bowl 'Sky Blue' and 'Deep Blue'

'Joker Light Blue'

'Maxim Marina' (purple to lavender-purple center)

'Mello 21' (bicolors)

'Oliver Twist' (yellow whiskered face, purple edge)

'Poker Face' (orange and purple bicolor)

'Rococco' (deep colors, ruffled edge)

'Watercolor' (pastels)

VIOLA

Cornuta 'White Perfection'

'King Henry' (Johnny-jump-up)

'Koreana Sylettas' (cyclamen leaved with lavender flowers)

'Plum Velvet'

'Sorbet Royale' (yellow and purple bicolor)

Sororia 'Freckles' (lavender-spotted)

'Yesterday, Today & Tomorrow' (white to light blue to deep blue)

ASPARAGUS

I always look forward to those clear spring mornings in early June when I head out with the dogs to harvest the daily crop of asparagus. My patch is not very large, so there is a bit of a hectic race between Pookie and me as to who gathers the most asparagus. I am sure he is the only dog who eats asparagus directly from the garden. He munches through the asparagus and raspberry patches, devouring whatever he can reach or what I do not get to first. Only because I love him so much do I let him get away with snatching what should be lunch. I am certainly not so generous with the deer, birds, and rabbits that try to share my vegetable garden. • Considering the competition, bringing a full basket of fresh asparagus into the kitchen is a simple but complete pleasure. As we move through spring, baskets of beans, tomatoes, onions, and fresh herbs make cooking and entertaining so much livelier and festive. But that first harvest of asparagus is perhaps the most enjoyable, as it signals the coming of summer. • My love of spring vegetables goes back again to my grandmother's huge asparagus beds. We picked batch after batch of asparagus, steamed them, and served them with either Grandma's delectable cheese sauce or simply butter and lemon. Since those days, I have had asparagus à la Française with Hollandaise sauce or vinaigrette. I've prepared a plateful of fat white asparagus with tons of butter and cracked pepper, as the Germans and Austrians do. I have puréed it, roasted it in olive oil, and then garnished it with fresh parmigiano. I've eaten big plump spears the size of cigars and slender ones no thicker than a knitting needle, made rustic soups served *en croûte*, and had wild asparagus. No matter how it is clothed, asparagus always tastes of spring to me.

Asparagus is best cooked the same day you buy it. If this is not an option, wrap asparagus tightly in a plastic bag and store it in the refrigerator. A second option is to store the asparagus standing upright in the refrigerator in a tall container with about an inch of water, and covered with a plastic bag. Asparagus can also be frozen, but it will lose some of its garden freshness. Frozen spears are fine for soups.

Perfectly fine results can be achieved without a steamer. Put about an inch of water in the bottom of a skillet, add salt, and bring to a boil. Lay the asparagus in the boiling water. Cover the pan until the water is boiling again, then immediately uncover it. Boil slowly for 3 to 5 minutes, or until crisply tender.

Asparagus can also be baked. Place the spears in a single layer in a shallow baking dish. Drizzle with olive oil—about 2 table-spoons for each pound of asparagus—and bake in a preheated 500° F. oven for 8 to 10 minutes. Season to taste with lemon juice, salt and pepper, or grated Parmesan cheese. Serve immediately.

The flavor of fresh asparagus also stands up to roasting, either alone or with a combination of other vegetables. Preheat the oven to 400° F. Snap off white woody bottoms and arrange one layer of asparagus in a roasting pan. Brush the stalks with olive oil and sprinkle with salt and pepper. Roast until lightly browned. Turn, brush again with olive oil, and roast until tender. Treat the aspara-gus the same way if grilling it on the barbecue.

As an option you can splash balsamic vinegar on before serving or add roasted hazelnuts or pecans. Simply toast the nuts in a medium frying pan over moderately low heat, stirring frequently, until golden brown (about 6 minutes). Or toast them in a 350° F. oven for about 8 minutes. Add the nuts to the roasted or grilled asparagus before serving and season with salt and pepper. A dash of roasted garlic oil also pairs well with grilled spears.

Although few of us need another specialized kitchen appliance, aspara-gus steamers—either glass or metal—do have their purpose. The woody bottoms of the standing asparagus cook more quickly than the tender tips when placed in steamers, resulting in an evenly cooked spear.

The asparagus at the farmer's market in Paris was so attractive that I decided to bundle it in silver baskets and use it as an instant table decoration. I bought the violets, already gathered in sweet nosegays, from the same market. Voilà! The spring luncheon table is complete.

TIP

If you must harvest your asparagus from the grocery store, look for spears that are firm, completely closed at the tip, and of uniform thickness. Although some prefer thin spears, fat spears are just as tender, especially if you gently peel from the butt end, cutting more shallow as you near the tip.

SALMON AND PAPPARDELLE WITH ASPARAGUS AND LEMON CREAM
Serves 6

    2   pounds thin asparagus, ends trimmed
    3   tablespoons butter
    ½   cup finely chopped shallots
        Juice and finely grated zest of one lemon
    1   cup rich chicken stock
    1   pint heavy cream
2 to 2 ¼ pounds skinless salmon fillet,
        cut into 6 serving-size pieces
    ½   tablespoon coarse salt
    2   tablespoons crushed black peppercorns
    1   tablespoon olive oil
    1   pound pappardelle pasta
    ½   cup chopped dill

1. Preheat broiler. Set a large saucepan of water to boil for the pasta. Cut asparagus into 2-inch lengths. In a large skillet of boiling water, boil asparagus until al dente, about 2 minutes. Drain and cool.

2. In a heavy, medium saucepan over medium heat, melt 2 tablespoons of the butter and sauté shallots until transparent, about 3 minutes. Add lemon juice, bring to a boil, and then reduce heat to simmer and cook for 2 minutes. Add chicken stock and cream and boil gently for 10 minutes, until slightly thickened. Set aside.

3. Season salmon with salt and pepper. Grease a broiling pan with olive oil. Place salmon on pan and broil for about 8 minutes (depending on thickness of fillet).

4. Cook pasta according to package directions. Drain pasta and toss with remaining tablespoon of butter and asparagus pieces and transfer to a large pasta bowl. Meanwhile, reheat the sauce and stir in lemon zest and dill. Pour the sauce over the pasta and serve immediately as an accompaniment to the salmon.

ASPARAGUS & LOBSTER CUSTARD
Serves 6

    1½ cups chopped asparagus, tips reserved
    5   eggs
    1   cup rich chicken stock
    1   cup milk
    ¼   cup fresh lemon juice
    2   tablespoons grated lemon zest
    ¼   cup plus 2 tablespoons grated Parmesan cheese
    2   cups coarsely chopped cooked lobster meat
        or crawfish

1. Preheat oven to 325° F. Place chopped asparagus, eggs, chicken stock, milk, lemon juice, lemon zest, and ¼ cup Parmesan cheese in a blender or food processor. Blend until smooth.

2. Divide lobster evenly into the bottom of six 10-ounce ramekins. Divide custard mixture among the six cups, pouring over the lobster. Divide asparagus tips among the six ramekins, and sprinkle the ramekins with the remaining Parmesan cheese.

3. Place ramekins in bain-marie (a large roasting pan with an inch of cool water) and bake for 25 to 35 minutes, or until custard is just set.

WHITE ASPARAGUS VINAIGRETTE MIMOSA

Serves 6

2 pounds white asparagus
1 garlic clove, finely chopped
½ teaspoon Dijon mustard
⅓ cup white wine vinegar
 Salt and freshly ground white pepper to taste
2 tablespoons chopped parsley
⅔ cup olive oil
2 hard-cooked eggs, finely chopped

1. Clean the asparagus and remove woody ends. Steam for 3 to 5 minutes (depending on thickness) or simmer in a skillet of water and drain well. Cool.

2. In a small bowl, whisk together garlic, mustard, vinegar, salt, pepper, and parsley. While whisking, add olive oil in a steady stream and continue to whisk until an emulsion is formed.

3. Pour vinaigrette over asparagus and marinate for 15 minutes. Garnish with chopped egg and serve.

ASPARAGUS SOUP

Serves 6 to 8

2 tablespoons olive oil
1 small leek, cleaned and chopped
1 small onion, chopped
2 medium russet potatoes, peeled and cubed
2 pounds asparagus, cut into 1-inch pieces, tips reserved
6 cups (plus) chicken stock
¼ teaspoon cayenne pepper, or to taste
1 tablespoon fresh lemon juice
½ cup heavy cream
 Salt and white pepper to taste
 Zest of 1 lemon

1. In a large saucepan on medium heat, heat olive oil and sauté leeks and onion for 3 minutes. Add potatoes and asparagus stalks and sauté for 5 minutes.

2. Add chicken stock and cayenne and simmer until potatoes are tender, about 15 minutes. Cool slightly.

3. In a separate pan, steam the asparagus tips for 2 minutes. Set aside.

4. Working in batches, purée cooled soup in a blender or a food processor (or purée in the saucepan with an electric handheld blender). Return soup to the pan, stir in lemon juice and cream, and add salt and pepper to taste. Simmer for 5 minutes, adding more stock if a thinner soup is desired. Add asparagus tips and serve garnished with lemon zest.

ASPARAGUS IN PUFF PASTRY WITH LEMON SAUCE
Serves 6

½ pound frozen puff pastry,
     thawed overnight in refrigerator
1 egg yolk mixed with 1 teaspoon water
36 thin asparagus stalks
     Juice of one lemon
2 sticks unsalted butter, softened
     Salt and white pepper pepper to taste

1. Preheat oven to 425° F. Unwrap puff pastry. On a lightly floured surface, roll out pastry to an 11-inch square, a scant ¼ inch thick. Cut pastry into 6 rectangles. Score pastry in a lattice pattern with a sharp knife. With a metal spatula, transfer rectangles to a cookie sheet and brush with beaten egg yolk, avoiding the edges of the pastry. Bake for 10 minutes or until golden. Cool.

2. Meanwhile, cut asparagus to about 3 inches long and cook in boiling, heavily salted water until al dente, 2 to 3 minutes. Drain.

3. In a small pan, heat the lemon juice over low flame. Add butter slowly, whisking all the time until the sauce becomes smooth and creamy. Do not let boil. Remove from heat and season with salt and pepper.

4. Cut puff pastry rectangles in half horizontally. Put cooked asparagus on the bottom half of the pastry rectangles. Pour lemon-butter sauce over each and top with the other half of pastry.

ASPARAGUS AND LEMON CONFIT
Serves 6 to 8 (makes about 1½ cups)

3 lemons
1 medium onion, chopped
¼ cup granulated sugar
½ pound asparagus, cut into ½-inch pieces
2 tablespoons parsley, chopped
     Salt and pepper to taste

1. With a paring knife, remove the zest from the lemons, leaving some pith on the skins. Reserve lemons. Julienne the zest. Put the zest in a small saucepan, cover with water, and boil for 5 minutes. Drain and cool.

2. Remove and discard as much pith as possible from the peeled lemons; discard pits. Chop lemons.

3. In a small saucepan on medium heat, combine onion, chopped lemons, julienned zest, and sugar. Bring to a boil. Reduce heat to simmer and cook for 5 to 7 minutes.

4. Add asparagus and cook an additional 5 to 7 minutes, until mixture thickens and asparagus are tender. Add parsley and salt and pepper and serve.

ASPARAGUS WRAPPED WITH VEAL AND PROSCIUTTO
Serves 6 to 8

    32 asparagus
     8 slices veal scallopini (18 ounces)
     8 thin slices prosciutto
    ¼ cup flour
     2 tablespoons unsalted butter
     3 tablespoons olive oil
     4 large shallots, chopped
     1 pound mushrooms, sliced
    ½ cup dry white wine
     1 cup rich chicken or veal stock
    ½ cup heavy cream
        Salt and pepper to taste

1. Clean and trim asparagus to 4 inches. Steam until slightly tender or cook in a skillet of boiling water for about 3 minutes. Drain, rinse under cold running water, and cool.

2. Lay out and flatten veal. Place a slice of prosciutto on top. Place 4 asparagus at the end of each slice of meat and roll up, securing with a toothpick.

3. Dredge each bundle in flour and shake off excess.

4. Melt butter and olive oil in a large frying pan over medium-high heat. Sauté scallopini bundles quickly to brown all over for 2 minutes. Remove and stack on a plate; cover with foil to keep warm.

5. In the same pan on medium-high heat, add shallots and sauté for 3 minutes. Add mushrooms and sauté another 5 minutes. Add white wine and boil 2 minutes, scraping up bits from bottom of the pan.

6. Add chicken stock and cream and lower heat. Simmer 5 minutes. Season with salt and pepper. Add asparagus bundles and simmer, turning with tongs until heated through, about 2 minutes. Remove toothpicks and serve immediately.

Option: Serve with extra asparagus and jasmine rice to soak up the sauce.

ASPARAGUS FONTINA TART
Serves 4

     8 ounces frozen puff pastry, thawed overnight
        in refrigerator
    ½ cup grated fontina cheese
 16 to 20 asparagus stalks, cut to 3½ inches
     2 tablespoons grated parmigiano reggiano

1. Preheat oven to 375° F. Unwrap puff pastry; on a lightly floured surface, roll out dough to a scant ¼ inch thick. Using a saucepan lid as a template, cut out an 8-inch circle of dough and transfer to an ungreased cookie sheet. Chill in refrigerator or freezer for 10 minutes. Lightly prick dough all over with a fork.

2. Cover pastry with grated fontina up to ½ inch of the pastry edge.

3. Place asparagus spears in a spoke with 3 or 4 asparagus tips in the center (*see photograph*).

4. Bake until puffed and golden, about 20 minutes. Remove from oven and sprinkle tart with parmesan. Return tart to oven and bake for 5 more minutes. Serve warm.

S P R I N G
W E D D I N G

Although I thoroughly enjoy weddings (I've even had a couple myself), I have noticed lately that the process of planning a wedding has become increasingly complex and, at times, overshadows the business at hand. I've also noticed that the longevity of the marriage is often in inverse proportion to the elaborateness of the ceremony. My response to this phenomenon: Stage a small wedding with a simple theme without sacrificing the celebratory feeling that is essential to all rites of passage. • When creating this wedding, I chose a cool but sunny day in early June. The ceremony was held outside under the moss-covered roof of my gazebo, tucked back into the woods. Every type of green imaginable from spidery ferns to velvety moss and newborn maple leaves provided a fairy-tale backdrop. Not wanting to compete with nature's perfection, I went with an overall green-and-white theme accented by punctuations of pink in the garland, the cake, and the flower girl's dress. The greens and flowers for the garland and center-piece came right out of the forest edge. The table was adorned in a green-and-cream broad-striped silk that echoed the woodland. I allowed two extravagances at the wedding: the tiered cake iced with marzipan replicas of the centerpiece, and the champagne.

W EDDING THEMES

When anyone asks me for tips on planning a wedding, or any party, my first question is always: What do you want to say? That answer will be the nut of your wedding theme. The next step is to choose the colors to express that theme. The colors can be based on your wedding dress or your bridesmaids' dresses, or can be borrowed from the seasons. Whatever colors you decide to base your wedding on, my one piece of advice is keep it simple. Stick to two, or at most three, complementary colors and coordinate the flowers, bridesmaids' dresses, wedding bouquet, attendants' gifts, decorations, and cake to share the same color theme. The color theme from this small spring woodland wedding is very understated: green and ivory with a scattering of icy blue on the attendants' gifts (*below left*), and pale pink for the flower girl's dress and bouquet. By taking the flowers from the woods, I avoided starchy formality. By adding accents of pink and blue, I kept the simple green and ivory from fading into the background.

personal notes:

Even the simplest wedding can cause exhaustion.
Try not to handle too many tasks in too little time.
Annie (*left*) was overwhelmed with fatigue before
the first slice of the cake—gloriously created by
Sylvia Weinstock—was cut.

Ostrich fern
(Matteuccia struthiopteris)

Peony 'Mr. Ed'

Unripe blueberries

Queen Anne's Lace.

Double mock orange
(Philadelphus 'Virginal')

Sweet pepperbush
(Clethera alnifolia)

Garden moss

Philadelphus pendulifolius

GATHER TOGETHER THE BEST OF THE WOODLAND AND SAY "I DO."

Various elements (*opposite*) from the woods and the perennial border were chosen for the bridal bouquet and centerpiece (*following page*).

The amount of flowers and greens needed to make the garland depends on its length. The garland pictured on the opposite page is 8 feet long. Gather enough greens to make three bunches per foot of garland. Each bunch should consist of two sprigs of unripe blueberry, two bunches clethra, and six sprigs of laurel. The heads of the gathered bunches should be about 4 inches across. You should also have about three sprigs of mock orange per foot of garland.

HOW TO MAKE
THE WEDDING GARLAND

Materials Needed

Clothesline or rope
1 spool of 22-gauge florist wire
Green florist tape
16 yards (for an 8-foot garland) of 1½-inch
  satin ribbon
Unripe blueberries
Pink mountain laurel in bloom (*Kalmia latifolia*)
Sweet pepperbush (*Clethra alnifolia*)
Double mock orange (Philadelphus 'Virginal')
Two 4-inch floral water picks per foot of garland

How To

1. Gather greens (2 sprigs of blueberry to 6 sprigs of laurel), breaking ends off stems as you go so that each bunch is about 7 inches long. Bind stems with florist tape.

2. Working from left to right, lay the bundle on top of the rope with the bloom ends facing left. Wrap wire tightly around rope and bundle (*see photograph*).

3. Continue to gather bunches and wire to rope, covering the stems of the previous bunch.

4. When the last bunch is in place, poke short stems of greens into the end of the garland to camouflage the wired stems of the last bundle.

5. Fill floral picks with water. Cut mock orange stems to about 4 inches and put stems in floral picks. Push the picks in the garland at an angle, about 2 picks per foot of garland.

6. Hang garland on hooks or nails and attach bows and ribbons (*see opposite*).

STRAWBERRIES & RHUBARB

Rhubarb, along with its cousin, sorrel, is the first edible harbinger of spring. As soon as the snow melts, I look for the pale pink knobs, shaped like a baby's fist, pushing through the soil. A month after rhubarb bears fruit, strawberries ripen. Although rhubarb rarely makes an appearance without its mate, I am not a big fan of the marriage (I have a suspicion that somewhere in the labs of Monsanto or Dow, plant geneticists are splicing the best of both to come up with the Strawbarb or the Rhuberry), nor am I willing to wait that long before I cut the rhubarb stalks. Attempts at growing my own big juicy everbearing strawberries have not been successful; the plants freeze, heave, and die during the winter. I've had much better luck with petite Alpine strawberries, also known as *fraise des bois*. We start Rugen Alpines from seed in the greenhouse during the winter and are picking the tiny berries by June. Rhubarb and strawberries also serve as impressive edible ornamentals. I have lined the herb garden outside the greenhouse with Alpine strawberries because I love the white blossom (or pink if you plant the charming 'Pink Panda') and tidy habit (they don't throw out runners). The fruit

is an incidental plus. I planted rhubarb, since I couldn't have massive swaths of gunnera, along the cascade by the pond where I can admire its big, heart-shaped, crinkled leaves and red stalks amid the fine foliage of spirea. As much as I love rhubarb and strawberries as fruit and plant, both serve as charming themes for table decorations (see the strawberry topiaries in the *Winter Notebook*), as well. Rhubarb and strawberries are hard workers.

I often use seasonal fruits and vegetables for decoration: tomato and basil in summer, pumpkin and squashes for fall, and strawberries for spring. The ruby-red flesh of the berries plays well against white porcelain, such as the Wedgwood soup tureen (*below left*) and paisley blue-and-white linens—a color combination (red, white, and blue) that has never lost its appeal. This luncheon table was quickly assembled; I dug a few strawberry plants out of the garden and repotted them in mini silver-plated cachepots (*bottom*). As props for name cards, I crowned small silver match holders with a wee nosegay of strawberry leaves topped with a single Alpine berry (*below right*).

TIP

Although Thomas Jefferson noted in his garden journal that rhubarb leaves were "excellent as spinach," the leaves of rhubarb contain a high concentration of oxalic acid, a poison to animals and humans. Because of its ability to remove iron compounds, oxalic acid is used commercially in metal polishes and stain removers. To restore the shine to dingy or burned pots and pans, scrub them with the leaves of rhubarb. But rinse well after scrubbing.

CELEBRATE THE STRAWBERRY SEASON
LUSCIOUS, RIPE,

WITH A MEAL THAT STARS THE
RUBY-RED FRUIT.

RHUBARB BARBECUE SAUCE

Makes 2 cups

The barbecue sauce can be used on ribs or chicken.

> 3 tablespoons olive oil
> 1 medium onion, chopped
> One 2-inch piece of fresh ginger, peeled and chopped
> 6 garlic cloves, chopped
> 2 cups, diced (½-inch) rhubarb
> ½ cup dark brown sugar
> ½ cup soy sauce
> ½ cup orange juice
> 1 teaspoon Thai chili paste (optional)

1. In a medium saucepan, heat olive oil. Sauté onion, ginger, and garlic over medium heat for 3 minutes.

2. Add rhubarb, brown sugar, soy sauce, and orange juice. Add chili paste according to taste. Cook over medium-low heat, stirring frequently, for 20 minutes. Cool and purée in blender or food processor.

Barbecued Baby-Back Ribs

Serves 6

> 4½ to 5 pounds baby-back pork ribs (3 slabs)
> 2 cups Rhubarb Barbecue Sauce

1. Divide each slab of ribs in two and smear each piece with the sauce. Seal in a plastic bag and marinate in refrigerator 4 to 6 hours or overnight. Cook on an oiled grill over medium-hot coals, turning occasionally, until browned and crusty (about 40 minutes).

STRAWBERRY PIE

Makes one 9-inch pie

> 1½ cups all-purpose flour
> ¾ cup (1½ sticks) butter
> 5 tablespoons powdered sugar
> 3 pints strawberries, cleaned and stemmed
> 1 cup granulated sugar
> 3 tablespoons water
> 3 tablespoons cornstarch
> 1 pint whipping cream (optional)
> 1 pint vanilla ice cream (optional)

1. Preheat oven to 350° F. Put flour, butter, and powdered sugar in the bowl of a food processor and pulse to combine, until the mixture is crumbly. (You may also combine the ingredients in a bowl with a wooden spoon.) Press lightly into a 9-inch pie plate or tart shell to evenly line the bottom and sides. Bake for 20 minutes and let cool.

2. Reserve one-third of the best berries for topping. Put the remaining two-thirds of the berries into a nonstick skillet and toss with the granulated sugar and cornstarch. Add 3 tablespoons water and crush with a potato masher.

3. Bring mixture to a boil over medium-high heat, stirring continuously. Reduce heat and simmer, stirring until the mixture becomes clear, about 5 minutes. Pour into the baked pie shell and arrange the reserved berries on top. Cool in the refrigerator. Serve with whipped cream or vanilla ice cream.

RHUBARB CRUNCH
Serves 12

3 cups all purpose flour
3 cups oatmeal (old-fashioned rolled oats)
2 cups light brown sugar
2 tablespoons ground cinnamon
1½ cups (3 sticks) butter, melted
6 cups chopped (½-inch) rhubarb
2 cups granulated sugar
3 tablespoons cornstarch
2 cups water
2 teaspoons pure vanilla extract
1 pint whipping cream (optional)

1. Preheat oven to 350° F. In a large bowl, combine the flour, oatmeal, brown sugar, and cinnamon. Add melted butter and mix well with a spatula.

2. Press half the mixture evenly into the bottom of a 9x13x2 inch baking dish. Sprinkle rhubarb over flour-oatmeal mixture.

3. Put sugar, cornstarch, water, and vanilla in a medium saucepan. Bring to a boil over high heat, stirring constantly. Lower heat and simmer for 1 or 2 minutes or until the syrup is clear. Pour syrup over rhubarb.

4. Beginning around the sides of the dish, spoon the remaining flour-oatmeal mixture all over the rhubarb.

5. Place dish on a foil-lined baking sheet to catch drips, and bake 40 to 45 minutes or until slightly brown and bubbly. Serve warm or cold, topped with fresh whipped cream.

STRAWBERRY RHUBARB SHERBET
Serves 8 to 10 (about 6 cups)

1 cup granulated sugar
1 cup water
1½ cups chopped (½-inch) rhubarb
1 pint strawberries, washed, stemmed and halved
1 teaspoon lemon juice

1. Combine all ingredients in a medium saucepan and simmer, partially covered, for 15 minutes, until fruit is very soft. Cool and refrigerate until chilled.

2. Process the mixture in an ice cream maker and freeze.

personal notes:

RHUBARB BREAD
Makes two loaves, each serving 8

1½ cups dark brown sugar
1 cup (2 sticks) unsalted butter, softened
1 egg at room temperature
1 teaspoon soda
1 teaspoon salt
1 teaspoon vanilla
1 cup whole milk at room temperature
2 tablespoons vinegar (distilled, white wine or cider)
3 cups all-purpose flour
1½ cups diced (½-inch) rhubarb
½ cup chopped nuts, such as pecans or walnuts

1. Preheat oven to 350° F. Grease two 8-inch loaf pans and line bottom of each with waxed paper.

2. With an electric mixer, beat together brown sugar, butter, and egg until creamy.

3. In a medium bowl, mix soda, salt, and vanilla and set aside. Add milk and vinegar to the soda mix. On low speed, gradually beat liquid mixture into the brown sugar mixture.

4. In 3 batches, fold in flour, rhubarb, and nuts. Mix well, but be sure not to overmix.

5. Pour batter into loaf pans. Bake for 60 to 65 minutes. Let cool in pans for 10 minutes, unmold, and cool on a rack.

STRAWBERRY RHUBARB TART
Serves 8

1 basic tart dough recipe (see opposite)
1 quart strawberries, washed and stemmed, left whole or halved if large
2 cups chopped (½-inch) rhubarb
1 cup granulated sugar
Finely grated zest of 1 orange
2 tablespoons flour

1. Preheat oven to 350° F. On a lightly floured surface, roll out half the dough into a 12-inch circle, about ⅛ inch thick. Line a 9½ x 1-inch tart pan with the dough.

2. In a large bowl, toss together the remaining ingredients and spread over the bottom of the tart shell.

3. Roll out remaining tart dough and cut into about fourteen ½-inch wide strips. Top tart with strips in a lattice pattern.

4. Line a baking sheet with foil and place on a rack below the tart to catch drips. Bake until lattice is golden, about 45 minutes. Cool and serve at room temperature.

RHUBARB STRAWBERRY PAVLOVA
Serves 10

> 7   egg whites
> 1½ cups superfine sugar
> 1½ teaspoons white vinegar
> ½   cup powdered sugar
> 1   cup diced (½-inch) rhubarb
> 1   quart strawberries, hulled and sliced
> ¼   cup granulated sugar plus 2 tablespoons
> 1   pint whipping cream, chilled
> 1   teaspoon pure vanilla extract

1. Preheat the oven to 275° F. Line a large, heavy baking sheet with aluminum foil; butter foil and dust with flour. With an electric mixer, beat egg whites until just firm. Beat on medium speed as you gradually add superfine sugar and vinegar. Beat until egg whites are stiff and shiny. Fold in powdered sugar.

2. Fill a pastry bag with meringue. Butter a cookie sheet and dust with flour. Pipe the meringue on the cookie sheet (*see photograph*) and build up sides to form a decorative case.

3. Bake meringue shell for 2 hours, or until slightly golden. Cool completely, peel off foil, and set on a large platter.

4. In a medium saucepan on medium heat, cook rhubarb, half the sliced strawberries, and ¼ cup granulated sugar, covered, for 5 minutes. Uncover and cook, stirring frequently, until fruit is reduced to 1½ cups sauce, about 15 minutes. Cool completely and refrigerate until chilled.

5. In a large bowl, whip heavy cream, vanilla, and remaining 2 tablespoons sugar until stiff peaks form.

6. Carefully fold rhubarb-strawberry sauce into whipped cream. Pour mixture into meringue shell. Top with the remaining strawberries and serve.

BASIC TART DOUGH

> 2½ cups all-purpose flour
>   Pinch of salt
> 1   cup (2 sticks) unsalted butter, chilled and
>   cut into small dice
> 3 to 4 tablespoons ice water

1. Put flour and salt into the bowl of a food processor and pulse 3 times to blend. Add butter and lightly toss with your fingers to coat pieces with flour. Pulse processor to cut in butter. Dough should resemble coarse cornmeal and butter pieces should be no larger than small peas.

2. Add ice water gradually by tablespoons through feed tube while pulsing machine. Dough will begin to clump into a ball.

3. Remove dough from processor and divide equally into two smooth disks. Sprinkle lightly with flour and wrap separately in wax paper. Refrigerate at least one hour or until ready to use. Let hard dough soften a few minutes before rolling out.
Note: Dough can be made a day ahead or sealed in plastic and frozen for up to a month.

PEONIES

After a dingy, rugged winter, the appearance of any old early-blooming thing—snowdrops, forsythia, winter aconites—is enough to make my spirits soar. I know that trotting along in their wake will be daffs, tulips, and crocuses, an event that has my right foot—the one that pushes the spade into the ground—tapping in anticipation. But none of these eager arrivals can compete with finding the first nub of a ruby-red peony sprout pushing up through the soil. This is not to say that I am mad for the plant, but I am delirious for the flower. During the short three weeks that the peonies are in bloom in the cutting garden, I am all over them . . . with scissors. Deep reds, haughty scarlets, flashy magentas, seashell pinks, virginal whites, and single-petaled Japanese varieties with vibrant exotic centers come into the house. Every room is brimming with masses of peonies in vases, bowls, and beakers. When I enter the room their sensual fragrance and exuberant blossoms overpower me like love at first sight. • Meanwhile, the first spring thunderstorm is brewing, not a problem for sturdy tree peonies, but a potential disaster for herbaceous ones. Once the rains hit, their top-heavy faces will be pressed into the mud. Solemnly, I apologize to the flowers for the coming rain. But—to misquote Lewis Carroll's "The Walrus and the Carpenter"—answer came there none. And that was scarcely odd, because I'd beheaded every one.

Peonies exist in two forms: herbaceous (*Paeonia lactiflora*) and tree (*Paeonia officinalis*), so called because their woody stalks do not die back in the winter. Both types of peonies bloom in the spring for 4 to 6 weeks, but are of little interest when not in flower. Peonies are reliably hardy in most parts of the United States from Zones 3 through 8, as long as the climate provides two months of freezing temperatures.

Tree and herbaceous peonies should be planted in late summer in the North and early fall in the South. If you are planting eyes from a divided plant, be patient. Herbaceous peonies do not like to be moved and may take a few years to recover. Tree peony propagation is slow and difficult, which is why they are expensive and should not be undertaken by an amateur. When planting peonies, look for tubers with three to five eyes; tubers with fewer or no eyes often rot in the ground. Tubers with more than five eyes fail to produce large flowers. Herbaceous rhizomes will need at least 3 square feet of space in sun (at least 5 hours a day) and should be buried 2 inches deep with a generous dose of compost or bone meal. Tree peonies can reach as high as 7 feet, depending on the variety, and should be planted 4 feet apart with 4 to 5 inches of soil covering the graft, recognized by the ridge on the stem. It is recommended that fertilizers be applied sparingly, if at all, because too much nitrogen can burn the roots and cause excessive spindly growth at the expense of flowers. (As a testament to their ability to bloom without much intervention, peonies can often be seen blooming at abandoned farms.) However, tree peonies love iron. Throw a few old nails into the hole when planting. Young plants of both varieties should be protected with a layer of mulch for the first two or three seasons, but after this they do not need any coddling. Peonies are usually unaffected by drought, since the roots grow deep into the ground.

Herbaceous peonies should be staked early in the season and the foliage allowed to grow up to cover the stakes. The first summer rain will weigh on the blooming heads, pushing them to the ground if they are not staked. Once the plant has flowered, deadhead the fading flowers so they do not sap strength from the plant. Cut back the foliage of the plant to the ground after the first killing frost.

Favorite Peonies

'Sarah Bernhardt' (seashell-pink double)
'Festiva Maxima' (white double with red streaking in center)
'Red Grace' (deep red double)
'Old Faithful' (rose red double)
'Kansas' (large watermelon-red double)
'Largo' (rose-pink guard petals, rose middle, and gold stamens)
'Salmon Surprise' (salmon-pink single with gold center)
'Mr. Ed' (cream double with rose blush)
'Elsa Sass' (pure white double)
'Vivid Rose' (deep pink double)
'Top Brass' (ivory guard petals, double pale-pink center)
'Glory Hallelujah' (double red)

personal notes:

TIP

Garden myth has it that peony buds will not open unless ants dine on the nectar of the bud. Not true. If you examine the peony bud you will see scales on the base of the young bud. The outside edges of the scales contain tiny extrafloral nectaries, or special glands that produce nectar. Ants are very fond of this nectar, which is made up of sugar, water, and amino acids. While the ants eat the nectar they repel insects that might attack the bud, but the peony would still blossom even if the ants weren't present.

Herbaceous peony flower forms come in three shapes: single (with 5 to 10 petals), Japanese (big outer petals and small center petals), and doubles. Doubles are further broken down into ball-shaped (globe-like double blossoms), bombs (single petals surrounding a carnation-like double center), and flower-in-flower doubles (double bloom overlaying another double bloom). Tree peonies are divided into two breeding styles: Chinese ("moutan" or "mudan"), large double blooms, and Japanese ("botan"), focusing on elegant single flowers. Most Japanese tree peonies have some Chinese genes in their background, so there is some overlapping of forms. Japanese propagators have not been diligent about recording stock and it is difficult to find named varieties at garden centers. Stick to specialty growers, such as Klehm, for the better cultivars.

PEONIES LIVE LONG, SUCCESSFUL LIVES. THERE ARE 300-YEAR-OLD BUSHES IN CHINA THAT STILL BLOOM FAITHFULLY EVERY SPRING.

Peonies in the cutting garden include varieties of unknown parentage (*top row, left and right*), as well as named acquisitions. 'Festiva Maxima' (*opposite*) is one of my favorites, as is 'Red Charm' (*top row, center*). *Bottom row*: 'Jan van Leeuwen' is a strong single white. 'Hermione' is a well-formed, mid-pink as is 'David Lee' with its stunning yellow stamens.

"BEAUTY IS NATURE'S BRAG, AND MUST BE SHOWN . . . WHERE MOST MAY WONDER AT THE WORKMANSHIP." —JOHN MILTON

When faced with a peony catalog, I find it difficult to find one flower that isn't beautiful. But I must restrain myself—the peony plants will find a home in the cutting garden and space is limited. *Top row:* 'Pink Parfait,' 'Festiva Maxima,' 'Felix Supreme.' *Middle row:* 'Sarah Bernhardt,' 'Hermione,' 'Top Brass.' *Bottom row:* 'David Lee,' 'Bridal Gown,' 'Cardinal's Robe.' *Opposite:* 'Reine Supreme.'

Each spring I fill my house with masses of peonies. There is nothing more sensual than their roselike scent, and nothing more spectacular than their over-the-top blowsy femininity. If I feel I have to rein in their sensuality, I will force them into topiaries made of floral foam (*opposite*). When decorating a less formal outdoor lunch (*top left*) I leave a bit of the foliage on the stem to give the arrangement a looser air. Even a small cup of alternating pale and mid pink peonies (*bottom left*) punctuated by a single leaf is charming but lush. But my favorite indulgence is an oversized bowl filled with every texture and color of peony (*bottom right*).

peonies mixed

Although my first love is peonies standing alone, I am willing to couple them with other flowers, if I must. *Below:* White dogwood blooms when the peonies peak and makes a handsome partner in a rustic basket. Unripe blueberries and euphorbia added texture. *Opposite top:* The delicate crepe paper–like blossom of a tree peony is complemented by pale lilacs. *Opposite bottom:* The basket of lilacs, tulips, peonies, snapdragons, annual phlox, and eucalyptus berries looks as if it escaped from the canvas of a seventeenth-century Dutch master. Both baskets were filled with plastic liners and built on a base of balled chicken wire for stability.

CREATING THE
POTAGER

When I arrived at Weatherstone seventeen years ago, there existed a small perennial border, a hemlock hedge, the remnants of a vegetable garden, and 59 acres of potential hay. A short row of Concord grapes on one side and a spotty patch of asparagus on the other flanked the vegetable garden. It was an anemic plot ripe with possibilities.

• Filled with great enthusiasm and a desire to balance my concrete-confined existence in New York City, I planted dreams of the garden's future. With professional help and guidance, the restoration project began. I sowed my first vegetable garden—as the termites were devouring the screened-in porch—with the food and flavors I'd liked since childhood, and I patterned the layout on Grandma Beaty's gardens back in Missouri. Of course, reality did not measure up to my well-intentioned wishes and desires. Now those nascent small successes and failures are a foggy memory, a blur of instructions, to-do lists, order forms, and envious visits to mature gardens. Although the gardening bug had taken grip, it wasn't until three years ago that I took the serious spiritual plunge into horticulture. I was touched with a grower's mania. It was at this point that I decided to completely redo my early efforts in the Weatherstone vegetable garden. I took a zillion pictures of the plot, analyzing it over and over with all of its warts. Two summers ago I started planning this garden just in my head, and then, finally, I committed to paper. Many, many plans bit the dust before I finally settled on the final layout.

The first limitation to building the potager was my exuberance. I wanted everything, but space was limited. The second limitation was more intimidating: the Deer Problem. My garden was like a salad bar for these pesky creatures. We quickly built two rustic wooden enclosures girded with heavy-gauge wire. Once the enclosures were in place, I decided to make early use of the soil by planting spring-flowering bulbs. I ordered 2,000 tulip bulbs, amazed that such a small plot could engulf such a sea. I planted the bulbs that fall with the naive hope that they would cooperate with consistent heights and blooming time. This was more difficult than I imagined. I sketched the layout for the garden outside the enclosures, intermingling vegetables and cutting flowers. By the time the first snow fell, the plant and seed orders were in the mail.

PLANNING AND PLANTING THE POTAGER

- *Choose a site that receives a full day of sun, is near the house, and is reachable with a hose.*
- *Determine soil type: clay, sand, or loam. Clay and sandy soils need organic matter such as peat moss, manure, or compost. Have soil tested for nutrient content and pH.*
- *Mark outlines of site with string and stakes.*
- *Remove sod or grass from site in one-foot square sections with a square-nosed shovel or a sod cutter. Compost sod squares.*
- *Add amendments to soil recommended in soil test and rototill at least 6 inches into topsoil. Remove rocks. Repeat tilling until top layer of soil is fluffy.*
- *Smooth soil level with a tined rake.*
- *Edge bed with a shovel, tossing soil away from the edge onto the bed, for a neater look, or line squares with Belgian blocks or brick.*

personal notes:

Preparations for defining the potager began in the winter as I scribbled various versions of the layout on graph paper. As soon as the ground was willing, I began the work of defining the boundaries of the garden, using wooden stakes and string to keep us in line.

I started propagating seed in the greenhouse in January. Throughout the winter and into early spring, we laid lines to define the lettuce and parsley checkerboard, fortressed by corners of tulips. After those initial lines were set out, I began two months of planting. I put in the first sowing of lettuces, then created bamboo teepees and trellises for the pole beans, tall peas, and tomatoes. After the hemp on the bamboo teepees was strung, the garden took on a Japanese air—very simple and pristine. Soon after the tulips emerged, I found that one side of the garden needed more structure and decided to outline the four principal quadrants (the potager part of the fenced garden) with stone Belgian blocks. (Eventually I would like to pave the T of the quadrants in old brick.) Once the blocks were laid out, looking very neat and tidy indeed, I realized that something was missing from the center of the quadrants. A focal point? Vertical interest? The needed visual fillip was supplied by the potter Guy Wolff: four 20-inch, rope-rimmed terra-cotta pots. The pots were placed in the center of each quadrant, and filled with fennel, ruby chard, and tiny magenta petunias. The last element to be placed in the garden—at the intersection of the quadrants—was a majestic martin house that I found while on a book tour in California. All the elements of the potager are now in place, and I am tending the profusion of fresh flowers and vegetables that make summer such a joy. As I stroll through the lush garden, I am in awe that not long ago it was once just a muddled doodle on graph paper. But wait. Over there. Maybe that zinnia shouldn't be quite so red? And there. Wouldn't a bold gray cardoon look better in those pots? And are the sunflowers shading the sweet peas? Why didn't I plant charantais melons in that space there? Next year I will do better. There is always next year.

TIP

To keep the Weatherstone salad bowl full, the potager must be productive as well as beautiful. Early in the season, I tear a few leaves off each lettuce plant, rather than cutting a whole head and leaving a gap in the checkerboard squares. Once the plants mature and are close to bolting, I cut the whole head.

AS I STROLL THROUGH THE LUSH GARDEN, I AM IN AWE THAT NOT LONG AGO THIS WAS ONCE A MUDDLED DOODLE ON GRAPH PAPER.

Baby cardoons (*left*) occupy corner squares. Delphinium and coreopsis (*right*) stand guard outside the potager gates. Nancy (*below and opposite*) harvests the first lettuces, chard, and radishes from the potager.

personal notes:

Since my horizontal space in the potager is limited, I am forced to rely on vertical space and grow up, not out. The architectural element the bamboo teepees and trellises bring to the garden is an added bonus. Even when the peas and beans are in their infancy, the bamboo supports look striking.

HOW TO BUILD A BEAN OR PEA BAMBOO TRELLIS

Materials Needed

9 8-foot bamboo poles (⅝-inch diameter)
Biodegradable twine or jute (about 400 feet)
28 metal tent stakes

How To

1. The trellises are built in 8-foot sections. If you want your trellis to be more than 8 feet, lash completed 8-foot sections together at the trellis ends.

2. Each 8-foot section is made from three Vs, one top horizontal support, and two side supports. Begin by assembling the Vs: With two poles, form an upside down V with the wide part of the V spread about 3 feet. Lash the tops of the two poles about a foot from their ends. Repeat for the other two Vs. Push the feet of the Vs into the ground (about 3 feet apart) until steady and secure.

3. To connect the three Vs, set a top horizontal support pole across the top of the Vs (in the crotch of the small Vs formed from the lashing) and bind with twine. Lash another support pole about 3 feet from the top of the horizontal support pole on each side of the teepee.

4. Beginning at the top horizontal pole, run 14 vertical lines of twine spaced about 6 inches apart in the following fashion. Lash one end of the twine to the top horizontal pole, knot it around the side support pole, and secure the other end with a metal tent stake pounded into the ground (following the lines of the trellis V). Be sure to keep the twine taut when tying it to the stake. Repeat on the other side (as if you were making a tent).

5. When the vertical lines are in place, begin running the horizontal lines. Secure one end of twine about 6 inches from the top of the end V joint. As you bring the twine across, tie the twine with a simple knot to each of the 14 vertical lines and the support poles, forming a checkerboard net. Continue down the V pole until you have tied about seven lines. Repeat on the other side of the tent.

6. You are now ready to plant peas or pole beans at the base of the teepee. After the beans or peas have been harvested, cut the twine, compost it, and store the poles until the next growing season.

· GARDEN JOURNAL

DATE: _

GARDEN LOCATION: _

PLANTS: _

_ _

_ _

_ _

_ _

_ _

_ _

_ _

_ _

_ _

COMMENTS / RESULTS: _

_ _

_ _

_ _

GARDEN JOURNAL

DATE: ______________________________

GARDEN LOCATION: ______________________________

PLANTS: ______________________________

____

____

____

____

____

____

____

____

____

____

____

COMMENTS / RESULTS: ______________________________

____

____

____

THE WEATHERSTONE TRAGEDY

I've often wished that life came equipped with a rewind button. If it were, I would rewind back to January 22, the day my house burned nearly to the ground. I was in New York at a meeting when I received a call from my assistant, Molly, nervously telling me that Weatherstone was on fire. I remember saying something calm and logical like the fire department will put it out and is everyone safe? I had no idea of the seriousness of the destruction until I arrived in Sharon two hours later and saw a huge plume of smoke hovering in the sky. Main Street was closed to traffic and the road was blocked by trucks from seven neighboring volunteer fire departments. At first sight, I knew the house was gone. Flames were shooting out of windows and the ridge beam was ablaze. Two firemen were on cherry pickers attacking the fire from the roof; five more were on the ground with hoses aimed at the enemy. The firefighters continued to battle the flames until nightfall, some stayed until the next morning to put out errant flashes. After dawn, when the smoke had literally cleared, I found that the back wooden wing of the house (the pantry, the kitchen, and the garage) had been saved, but all that remained of the main part of the house was a stone shell open to the sky, filled with soggy, blackened rubble. No one had been injured, the dogs were unharmed, but I felt as if a part of my soul had died. I wanted to press the rewind button, to go back and stop the fire. My rational mind knew that the fire was caused by faulty wiring, that it had burned inside the walls undetected far too long to have been stopped by any one person. But my irrational mind, which was in shock, wanted to press that rewind button. It took me about a week to pull out of the numbing haze. There was work to do. Decisions to make. Insurance agents to appease. Fast-forward to spring. It was time to rebuild. My broken heart had mended after a few heavy doses of optimism. I had found an architect well versed in Classicism whose ideas and vision mirrored mine. We bonded as ideological kin. Since Weatherstone had been completely refigured and remodeled in 1915, there was little left of the original configuration of 1765 to be faithful to. I was free to reinvent the house, and as a result, to reinvent my soul. I have never been so excited by a project, never so full of such a strong sense of renewal. In a year the house will be finished and spring will have come again.

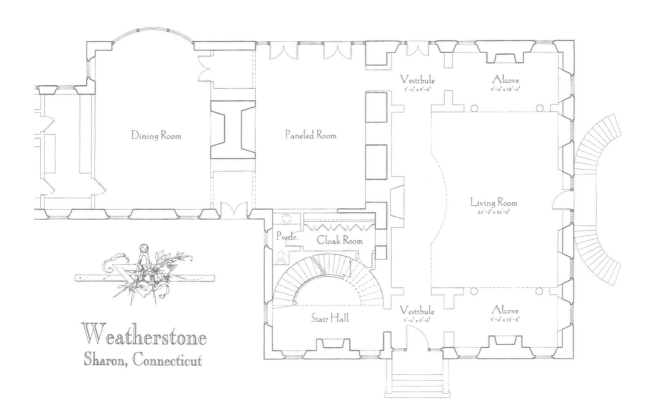

New plans show the most damaged part of the house reconfigured. The former library, center hall, reception room, and second-floor bedrooms will be transformed into a two-story 52-by-30-foot great room supported by Doric columns below and Ionic columns above. The second-story gallery of the great room will be dedicated to my love of books and lined with shelves.

A TIME OF RENEWAL

When I was young, the change of seasons had an entirely different meaning. Summer marked an endless three-month holiday, fall was back-to-school time, and winter brought a preoccupation with Santa Claus. As I have gotten older, seasons no longer mean new clothes, freedom from schoolbooks, or material goods. Seasons have become far more profound. Especially spring. As a metaphor, spring has taught me to believe in the inevitability of renewal. No matter how grim the winter, no matter how many setbacks I have endured, the earth will come alive again in a glorious display of optimism. Watching the coming of spring is, to me, to observe a miracle of reinvigoration, despite a lifetime of experience proving that miracles are hard to come by. Spring is one of life's only immutable acts of joyful continuity. I know that every April, until I run out of Aprils, the garden will come back to me, the apple trees will blossom and the robins will return. When I was small, spring's dependability meant nothing to me, but, of course, then I was immortal as all young people are. Now that I have more gardening seasons behind me than I have ahead, I have come to count on spring's reliable glad tidings. I couldn't ask for a better friend.

CONTRIBUTORS

This is **Sylvie Becquet**'s fifth outing as principal photographer. Paris-based Sylvie has become accustomed to jet lag without complaint. **Alan Richardson**, as usual, is right on target and in focus. Word of warning: Don't mess with his perfectly poached egg. **Melissa Davis** sharpens her pencil and wits in anticipation of book number five, *At Home*, to be published in the winter of 2000. Despite the inconvenience of giving birth during deadlines, **Dina Dell'Arciprete** trudged ahead with style and baby Austin at her side. After six years as head gardener at Weatherstone, **Nora Holmes** departs for greener pastures to Mole's Hill Farm. We will miss her prowess with a spade. Weatherstone chef **Nancy Quattrini** proclaims that she has not exhausted her repertoire of asparagus recipes. However, she recently threatened us with a passion for galangal. **Placido** and **Margarida deCarvalho** continue to carry on with efficiency and good humor during the rebuilding of Weatherstone. Placido has taken on the added responsibility of Estate Manager/Geese Terrorist with aplomb. While continuing to help with flowers and other projects, **Susan Poglitsch** grapples with the impossible title of Head Puppy Wrangler with the goal of keeping Ruffie under control. Personal assistant **Molly McCarthy** tells me what I can and can't do and when I can and can't do it. I'm pleased to report that she's eating meat again but still has that condiment problem. **Rosa Costa**, the Uber-Organizer, keeps things running smoothly in New York while juggling the phones for *Carolyne Roehm Home*. Many thanks to **Diana Sturges**, who took the heat and stayed overtime in the kitchen to test the *Notebook* recipes. **Annie** and **Pookie** have been teaching the new dogs **Winnie** (cairn terrier) and **Ruffie** (wheaten terrier) how to garden. The new dogs are especially adept at digging up newly planted perennials and bulbs. The dogs are oblivious to the pesky swarms of geese settling on the pond, but are ferociously hostile toward the carp.

SOURCE GUIDE

DAFFODILS

The American Daffodil Society, Inc.
4126 Winfield Rd.
Columbus, OH 43220-4606
$20 membership includes receiving the
quarterly magazine, *The Daffodil Journal.*

Van Engelen & Scheepers
23 Tulip Drive
Bantam, CT 06750
Tel: 860-567-8734
Fax: 860-567-5323
www.vanengelen.com

Brent and Becky's Bulbs
7463 Heath Trail
Gloucester, VA 23061
Tel: 804-693-3966
Fax: 804-693-9436
www.brentandbeckysbulbs.com

Van Bourgondien Brothers
P.O. Box 1000
245 Route 109
Babylon, NY 11702
Tel: 516-669-3500
Fax: 516-669-1228
www.dutchbulbs.com

EASTER

Chris' Topiary Nursery
9004 Copley Ln.
Riverside, CA 92503
Tele: 909-352-3526
http://members.aol.com/MrTopiary
Topiary bears and other shapes.

Fouquet Chocolatier Confiseur
22 rue François 1er
Paris 75008
France
Tel: 01.47.23.30.36
email: info@fouquet.fr
Sugar bunnies.

MOTHER'S DAY

Scully & Scully
504 Park Ave.
New York, NY 10022
Tel: 212-755-2590
Fax: 212-486-1430
www.scullyandscully.com
Trays.

Christian Dior
712 5th Ave.
37th Floor
New York, NY 10019-4108
Tel: 212-582-0500
Fax: 212-582-1063
Trays.

TULIPS

Breck's of Holland
6523 North Galena Rd.
Peoria, IL 61632
Tel: 309-689-3860
Fax: 800-996-2852
http://www.gardensolutions.com

Dutch Gardens
P.O. Box 200
Adelphia, NJ 07710
Tel: 800-818-3861
Fax: 723-780-7720
www.dutchgardens.com

PANSIES

Two's Company
30 Warren Place
Mt. Vernon, NY 10550
Tel: 1-800-896-7266
Silver beakers.

ASPARAGUS

Miller Nurseries, Inc.
5060 West Lake Rd.
Canandaigua, NY 14424
Tel: 800-836-9630
Fax: 716-396-2154
jmiller@millernurseries.com
Purple and green asparagus roots.

SPRING WEDDING

ABC Carpet & Home
888 Broadway
New York, NY 10003
Tel: 212-473-3000
Green-and-white fabric:
Scalamandre's Canal Stripe.

Sylvia Weinstock Cakes Ltd.
273 Church St.
New York, NY 10013
Tel: 212-925-6698
Fax: 212-925-5021

Web Sites
http://www.weddings-
online.com/wed/Timeline.html
A month-by-month checklist
for planning your wedding.

STRAWBERRIES & RHUBARB

Nourse Farms, Inc.
41 River Road
South Deerfield, MA 01373
Tel: 413-665-2658
Fax: 413-665-7888
www.noursefarms.com

Ornamental Edibles
3622 Weedin Court
San Jose, CA 95132
Tel: 408-946-7333
Fax: 408-946-0181
www.ornamentaledibles.com
Alpine strawberry plants.

Indiana Berry & Plant Co.
5218 West 500 South
Huntingburg, IN 47542
Tel: 812-683-3055
Fax: 812-683-2004

Bergdorf Goodman
754 Fifth Avenue at 57th Street
New York, NY 10019
Tel: 212-753-7300
Hartley Greens & Co. creamware.

La Boutique
Château de Bagnols
69620 Bagnols, France
Tel: 33 (0)4 74 71 4000
Fax: 33 (0)4 74 71 4049
http://www.bagnols.com/boutique/home.html
Silver scalloped beakers and other items
to order on-line.

PEONIES

Klehm Nursery
4210 N. Duncan Rd.
Champaign, IL 61821
Tel: 217-359-2888
Fax: 217-373-8403
www.klehm.com
Offers a large selection of
herbaceous and tree peonies.

Golden Port International
2255 Cedars Road
Lawrenceville, GA 30043
Tel: 1-877-736-6437
Fax: 770-277-9510
http://www.goldenport.com/peony